Homes on Wheels

Heather Hammonds

Chapter 1

Homes on Wheels

Have you ever seen a home on wheels?

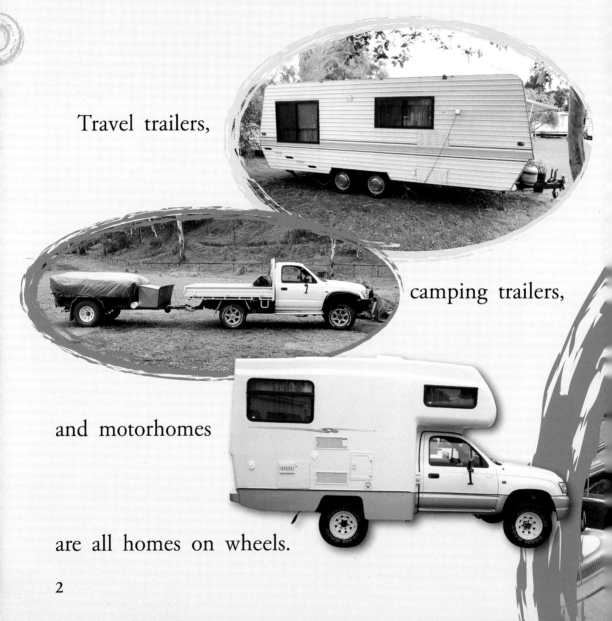

Travel trailers,

camping trailers,

and motorhomes

are all homes on wheels.

Homes on wheels can be moved from place to place.

You can live in them for a few days when you are on vacation, or you can live in them all the time.

Travel trailers, camping trailers, and motorhomes are also called RVs, or **recreational vehicles.**

Travel Trailers

Travel trailers are pulled along by a car or truck.

Some travel trailers have two wheels.

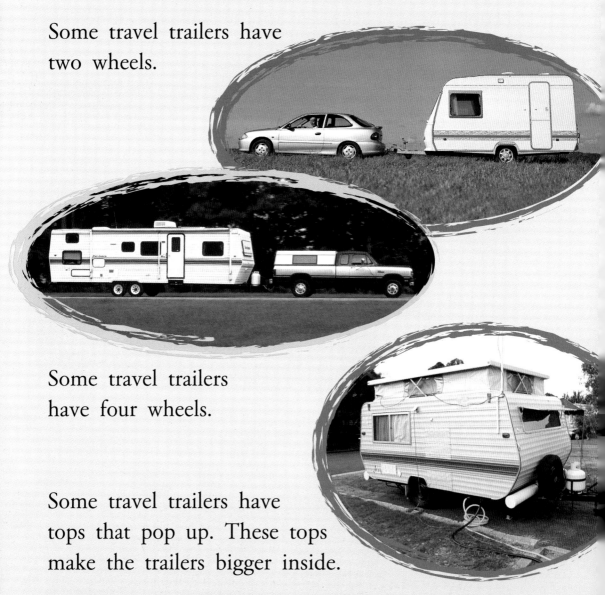

Some travel trailers have four wheels.

Some travel trailers have tops that pop up. These tops make the trailers bigger inside.

Camping Trailers and Motorhomes

Camping trailers are pulled by a car or truck, too. The top of the camping trailer is put up when it is parked.

Motorhomes are not pulled by a car or truck. Motorhomes have their own **engines**.

When travel trailers or camping trailers are pulled along by a car or truck, they are being **towed**.

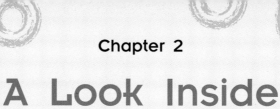

Chapter 2

A Look Inside

All travel trailers, camping trailers, and motorhomes have a place to sleep and eat inside them.

This small travel trailer has a stove for cooking. It has cabinets and a table and a seat that turns into a bed.

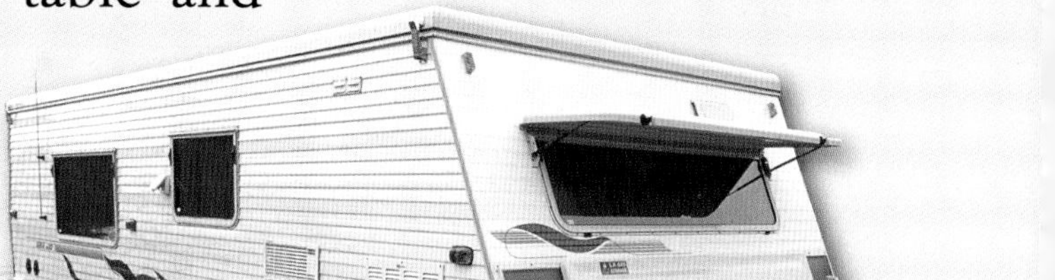

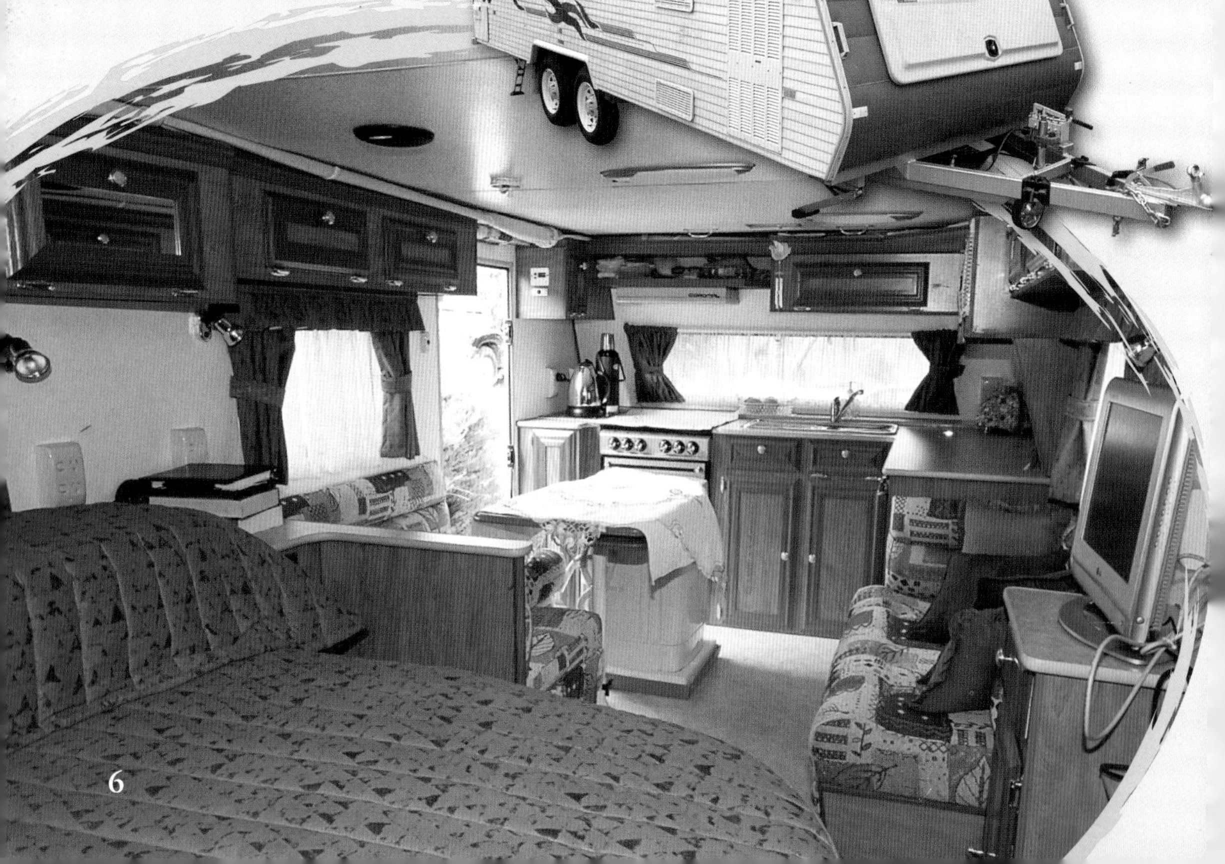

This big motorhome has a bedroom, a kitchen, a bathroom, and a living room.

Chapter 3

Traveling Safely

It is important to stay safe when traveling with a home on wheels.

Special parts are used to hook this travel trailer to the car. The parts are strong so the travel trailer stays attached to the car.

safety chains

tow bar

When this travel trailer is moving, no one goes inside it. Everyone stays in the car with their seat belts on.

This big motorhome travels slowly on the road. The driver watches for smaller cars around him.

It is best to drive slowly on windy days when pulling a travel trailer or camping trailer. Travel trailers and camping trailers can get blown about by the wind.

Chapter 4

Vacation Fun

When you go on vacation with a travel trailer, camping trailer, or motorhome, you can:

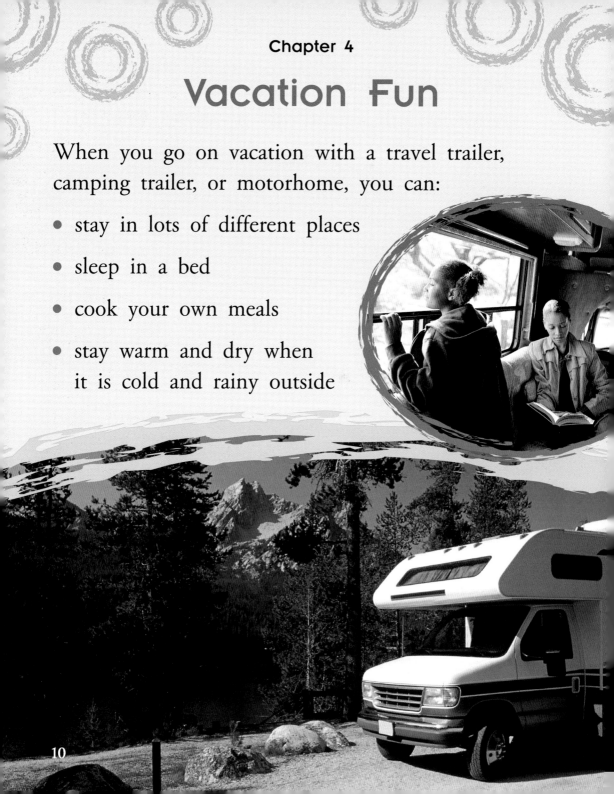

- stay in lots of different places

- sleep in a bed

- cook your own meals

- stay warm and dry when it is cold and rainy outside

Some people have their own travel trailer, camping trailer, or motorhome. Other people **rent** a home on wheels.

Travel trailers, camping trailers, and motorhomes can be rented in lots of different countries.

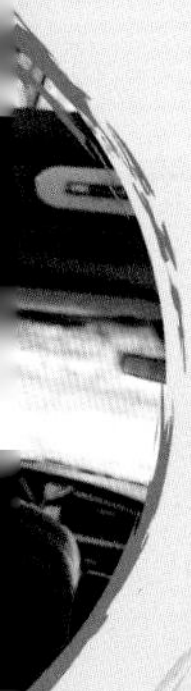

Motorhome Rental

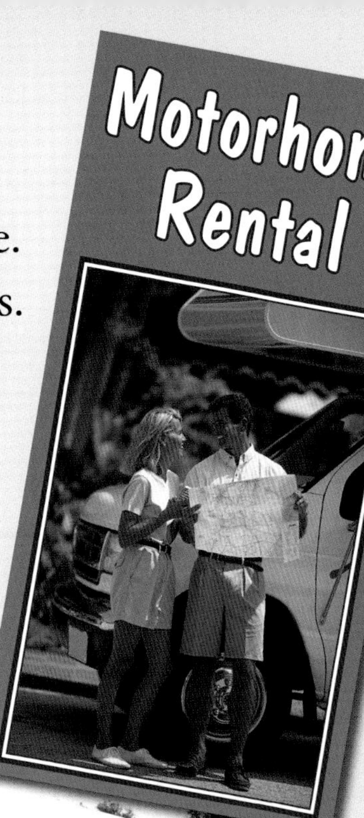

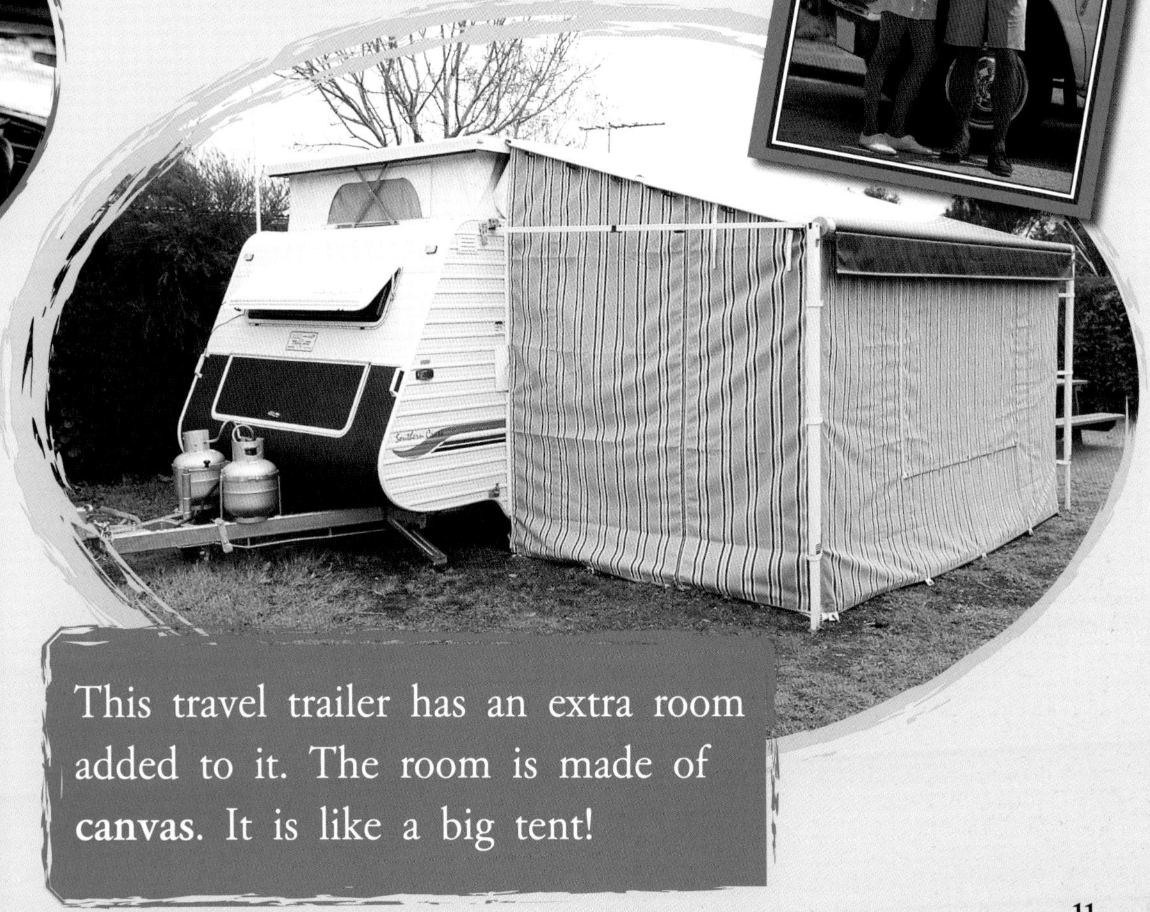

This travel trailer has an extra room added to it. The room is made of **canvas**. It is like a big tent!

Most people stay in RV parks with their homes on wheels.

Before they go on vacation, they decide where they will stay. They may stay in one RV park, or they may travel to different RV parks.

RV parks have:

- **electricity** for lights, stoves, televisions, and other machines

- water

- bathrooms

- a store

- places to play

RV parks can be found at the beach, in the mountains, and other places people like to visit when on vacation.

Chapter 5

Year-Round Living

Many people live in their homes on wheels all year around.

These people live in their big motorhome all the time. They travel to lots of beautiful places. They make new friends along the way.

These people live in their travel trailer all the time. They keep their travel trailer at an RV park. They have many friends at the RV park.

Chapter 6

Clubs and Shows

Many people who travel in homes on wheels join an RV club. Club members often travel together to different RV parks. They enjoy showing others the best places to stay.

It is also fun to visit RV and camping shows.

The latest recreational vehicles can be seen at RV and camping shows.

Tents and other outdoor equipment can be seen at RV and camping shows, too.

Chapter 7

Circus Wheels

This circus travels from place to place all year.

The people who work in the circus live in travel trailers and motorhomes.

They travel with the circus in their homes on wheels.

Some circus travel trailers are very big. They are pulled from place to place by trucks.

The animals in this circus have homes on wheels, too!

CIRCUS ELEPHANTS

Chapter 8

Vacations with a Horse

Long ago, homes on wheels were pulled by horses. Today you can still go on a vacation in a **horse-drawn** trailer.

You can hire a horse-drawn trailer and travel to beautiful places.

Horse-drawn trailers go very slowly. They cannot go as fast as a trailer that is pulled by a car or a truck. It takes much longer to go from place to place.

Long ago some people lived in horse-drawn trailers.

Chapter 9

Moving On

Recreational vehicles of today look very different from homes on wheels of long ago.

This old travel trailer was made of wood.

This old travel trailer looked very shiny.

What will new kinds of recreational vehicles look like?

Glossary

canvas	a kind of thick material, often used to make tents
electricity	a kind of power used to run lights, stoves, and other machines
engines	machines inside cars or trucks that make them move
horse-drawn	pulled along by a horse
recreational vehicles	kinds of transportation people use when they are on a vacation or having fun
rent	to pay money to borrow something
towed	pulled along

Index